How to Run Awesome Discovery Sessions:
Modern, Agile JAD-like Sessions

By **Trond Frantzen**

Cataloguing-in-Publication Data

Copyright © 2015 by **Trond Frantzen**.

How to Run Awesome Discovery Sessions:
Modern, Agile JAD-type Sessions

1. Business requirements solicitation
2. System requirements solicitation
3. JAD sessions
4. Business system analysis
5. Requirements analysis Discovery Sessions

You can reach Trond Frantzen at the e-mail address below:

Trond.Frantzen@PowerstartGroup.com

Good Words

"The business requirements sessions were a great success. I am grateful I had the opportunity to participate in many of the discovery sessions, and must tell you it was a pleasure working together to define our requirements. It has created an air of excitement in our office."

● Director, Insured Health Services

"Trond is an exceptional individual who can provide any organization with insights they would otherwise not discover about themselves. He is an expert at dragging business requirements and information out of clients that they did not know they even knew."

● Gord Kargus – Senior Partner
B-diligent Business Solutions Corporation

"Trond has a magical quality. I have seen his work take very complex disasters and using his approach, create a project that has everyone nodding yes to. We all tend to complicate the heck out of everything and Trond has a knack of getting to what is needed vs wanted. Simplification and segmentation of events is the making of a successful project and a happy CFO."

● John Nesbitt – SVP, Business Development
Pathway Communications

The Book

About the Author

Trond Frantzen has over 30 years of experience as a business leader, an IT consultant, an author and coaching leader. He founded two international companies: The PowerStart Group and PowerPlus Systems Corporation. He developed the primary analysis methodology and led the consulting team of both these companies over the past 30 years.

He is the author of six best-selling business books, developed a multi-million dollar business, and has delivered strategic consulting services to scores of clients; and conducted

 interactive courses and seminars with over 35,000 people.

Trond was born in Norway, raised in Toronto's west end, graduated from Concordia University, lives in Calgary, and is connected to a very large social network of friends.

As a professional with many years of business development experience, and a finalist in the *Entrepreneur of the Year* Oakville Awards of Business Excellence, Trond has been recognized by many professional associations.

Trond's passion is investing in the success of others – people, organizations and his community.

You can connect with Trond on LinkedIn at
http://www.linkedin.com/in/trondfrantzen

What's This Book All About?

I've been studying and teaching Business System Analysis for many years. I've delivered courses and seminars to over 35,000 professionals. I've had a lot of fun. And I hope others have too.

At the end of the day, the only way you can "do" Business System Analysis is to actually get together with clients, users, subject-matter experts and ask them what it is they need for their system. Sounds straight-forward. But we all know it isn't. If it was, everyone would be doing it, without any big deal, and our business system requirements would be a breeze. But it just ain't so.

In my courses and seminars I spend a lot of time addressing how to go about doing the business requirements analysis. I demonstrate. We do workshops. We deal with the theories and practices. We do more workshops.

But the reality is, a classroom course or a seminar is not the real world. And we can never spend enough time on the foundations and principles ... the "how do I do this" ... of sitting down with clients, users and subject-matter experts.

This book ... is about the "how do I do this" of sitting down with clients, users and subject-matter experts, to figure out what they really want and need for their system.

This book ... will put into context the nature of your questions, the environment you need, how long it takes, who should be involved, and the tools you need.

You'll also learn how to do it quickly, without missing a thing.

You'll really find out what "agile" means – with the results, the specifications, the documentation; but without the chaos.

So let's get started.

What is a Discovery Session?

A 'requirements discovery session' is an interactive approach to conducting meetings with clients and subject-matter experts to probe and establish a project's business or organizational requirements. These highly interactive sessions include clients, business partners, subject-matter experts, business analysts, executives and some system professionals. But not necessarily everyone at once.

These discovery sessions are based on the sound, old principles of JAD, but with greater flexibility and more suited to the 21st century. The Discovery Sessions we're going to explore are much more complete, and faster than conventional JAD or even RAD sessions.

What's RAD and JAD?

Joint Application Development or Joint Application Design (known as JAD) was developed by Chuck Morris of IBM Raleigh (North Carolina) and Tony Crawford of IBM Toronto (Canada) in the late 1970's; the early, chaotic days of system development. In 1980 Crawford and Morris taught JAD in Toronto, and Crawford led several workshops to prove the concept. It worked well. The results were encouraging and JAD became a well-accepted approach in many enthusiastic organizations. In time, JAD gained general industry approval as a best practice.

Tony Crawford defines JAD as an interactive systems design concept involving discussion groups in a workshop setting. It has specific steps to follow. Originally, JAD was designed to bring system developers and users of varying backgrounds and opinions together in a productive and creative environment. The meetings were a way of determining system requirements and specifications.

Rapid Application Development (RAD) is based on JAD, but moves along faster by applying the 80/20 Rule in development and scope selectivity. 80/20 meant that they didn't sweat the small stuff … which also meant they missed a few things, since figuring out what was "small stuff" was very subjective.

What's it good for?

Requirements Discovery Sessions produce great savings by shortening the elapsed time required to gather business system requirements and by improving the completeness and quality of the requirements gathered. This reduces significantly the number of costly downstream requirements changes. Requirements Discovery Sessions have been extremely successful with many organizations worldwide, private and government alike. I've led scores of them, and consultants from my company have led them on over 850 projects.

However, the success of a requirements discovery session is not just a function of the business analysis methodology you use, it requires a well-practiced professional to lead the sessions and the unreserved, enthusiastic participation of clients, business partners, subject-matter experts and executives. In other words, there must be a real commitment by the organization's client base, not just fuzzy words of support. "Real commitment" means putting in the time necessary to participate in Discovery Sessions.

To be clear, that "real commitment" is a lot less than the time required by conventional analysis methods.

There are two kinds of requirements discovery sessions: the *Project Scope Blitz* and the detailed Discovery Session. We will discuss both.

The risks and rewards of Discovery Sessions

There are two major risks when planning requirements discovery sessions. Whether the discovery session is intended to be a front-end *Project Scope Blitz* or a series of regular detailed Discovery

Sessions, there are often unrealistic productivity expectations (a) before the discovery session, and (b) after discovery sessions.

When an organization embarks on a series of Discovery Sessions without being fully committed to the highly interactive nature of these sessions, it can fail or fall short of the mark. But if an organization devotes the right amount of time and the right people, the results will be substantial. Some of the benefits of a requirements discovery session include:

- It accelerates the business requirements learning process.

- It massively increases productivity by shortening the iteration cycle.

- It accelerates the business revitalization and process re-engineering process.

- It ensures the highest quality possible, because of direct participation by clients and subject-matter experts.

- It ensures the most complete business requirements analysis in the shortest period of time.

- It helps to develop mutual respect between business system analysts and clients.

- It provides a forum for exploring focused, in-context business revitalization ideas.

- It helps to deliver what the client needs and wants, quickly.

- It opens the door to success.

How the requirements Discovery Session is conducted is what sets it apart from other approaches to gathering business requirements. Critical ingredients for a successful Discovery Session include leadership from a trained and experienced practitioner and an expert scribe (also a business specialist); as well as participation by executive sponsors, key decision makers and *real* subject-matter experts; and the ability to work without the usual daily interruptions. Discovery Sessions can last anywhere from an hour to several days, depending on the critical nature of the project. Discovery Sessions should be uninterrupted, as much as possible, since the absence of key people delays progress.

And what's a *real* subject-matter expert? A *real* subject-matter expert (SME) has in-depth practical knowledge of the business areas affected by the project, and their work processes. This person also understands why work processes are organized the way they are, and what these processes are intended to achieve. This is not a surrogate "user"; nor is it a recent business school graduate who can fill the gap.

What is ... the Project Scope Blitz?

Every project has to start with one of these. To make it work well, you have to gather all project stakeholders together for about a half-day. The objectives of a Project Scope Blitz are as follows:

- To quickly identify many of the *business events* that will be part of the target system. (I will define a *business event* soon.)

- To determine the business areas or departments that have responsibility for responding to and dealing with the identified *business events*.

- To accurately predict the amount of time required to complete the detailed Discovery Sessions with clients and subject-matter experts, and to prepare the Business Requirements Document.

- To establish priorities – what *business events* will be done first, and which ones will be done later.

- To enable planning the schedule for detailed Discovery Sessions with clients and subject-matter experts.

- To determine the effort and cost of the project's business system requirements analysis.

What are ... detailed Discovery Sessions?

For each *business event*, there will be a detailed Discovery Session. The objectives of a detailed Discovery Session are as follows:

- To quickly get subject-matter experts on the same page, at the same time.

- To quickly uncover and discover the project's business requirements for one or more *business events* in a single session with one or more subject-matter experts.

- To enable the business system analyst to focus on a small component (a *business event*) and to quickly learn about the business requirements in support of that *business event*.

- To discover complete and accurate business requirements, focused and in context – not just "goodness and light".

- To achieve "buy-in" and ownership from clients and subject-matter experts.

- To develop mutual respect by all participants – subject-matter experts and business system analysts.

How long does a Discovery Session take?

Project Scope Blitz sessions usually take about a half-day, sometimes a little more. For an average project, if the client has a good handle on what they need, a half-day session is often enough.

It's important before planning a project's regular detailed Discovery Sessions to estimate how many *business events* there will be and how much time is needed for each one. How do you do that? Well, we'll discuss that a little later.

You also need to know who should participate – clients and subject-matter experts.

The **Project Scope Blitz** is very interactive with clients and subject-matter experts. It involves extracting from them the things they believe should be within the scope of the project. Our experience is that the more senior the participants are, the better your results will be.

We'll look at what a *business event* is a little further on in the book. For now, suffice it to say that a *business event* is a <u>situation</u>, <u>condition</u>, <u>circumstance</u> or <u>external requirement</u>. It is not a process. A process is what we do to supports a *business event* – a specific situation or circumstance that your system has to deal with.

When you start up a **Project Scope Blitz**, you can start by asking the participants about some of the things they need to have in their new business system. Their answers will not be in the form of *business events*. It's up to you, as the analyst, to distill what they say and turn it into *business event* statements.

Each time you identify a *business event*, it must be listed and clearly displayed so the participants can see what you are doing, and they can read the *business event* statement as you have written it. My preferred method is to write the *business event* statements with a dry-erasable marker on *Write On – Cling On* sheets which stick to the wall. Google this to find out more.

You can also use higher technology, involving a projector. If you capture *business event* statements in a document, you can project them onto a wall for everyone to see. The important point is, everyone gets to see what's being documented, which is really important. In this way, they can see what you hear.

One approach that I recommend when conducting a *Project Scope Blitz* is to create a short list of *business events* yourself, in advance, and then present these as "potential events" to your clients and subject-matter experts. It's very important to suggest them strictly as "potential events" since participants are more likely to buy-in to their own knowledge and contributions than to yours. This approach is particularly useful if you don't have much information about the project, or when the project deals with something that's new or different.

The whole idea behind this use of "potential events" is to stimulate participation from your clients and subject-matter experts who are part of the *Project Scope Blitz*.

In the early part of any interactive session, people are often hesitant to say anything or to get the ball rolling. If this is the case, then it's easy for you to toss out a "potential event" and to ask participants if that *business event* is something that could be part of the scope of the project. The answer could be a blunt *"no"*, in which case you strike it from your list.

After completing a *Project Scope Blitz*, you will have either a long or short list of *business events* for the project. There's no doubt you will <u>not</u> have discovered all of the required *business events*, but you will have enough to get you started.

Graphically, it would look like the picture below.

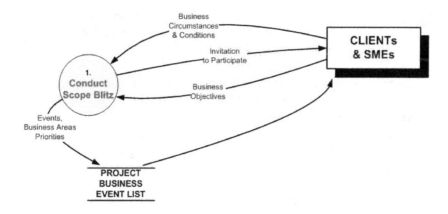

The process is as follows:

1. Determine the best time to conduct a **Project Scope Blitz**.

2. Issue a **Scope Blitz Discovery Invitation** to all clients and prospective subject-matter experts.

3. At the scheduled time, conduct the **Project Scope Blitz** with clients and subject-matter experts.

4. During the **Project Scope Blitz** with clients and subject-matter experts, determine the *business events* that are in-scope (as many as possible, but apply the 80/20 Rule, since other *business events* will be found during the detailed Discovery Sessions).

5. Record *business events* that are mentioned but are out-of-scope.

And, finally, issue the **Project Business Event List** to all participants as soon as practical after the **Project Scope Blitz**. The Blitz itself should take half-day or a full day. It is very, very rare that it takes more time.

If you would like to receive a set of almost 4,000 business events from over 850 projects, organized by business type, just send me an email to trond.frantzen@PowerstartGroup.com.

Once the **Project Scope Blitz** has been done, you will need to plan and schedule the **detailed Discovery Sessions**. This can get very interesting since you'll have to deal with the random availability of people, and coordinating the attendance of (usually) several people ... which means juggling vacations, conflicting meetings, time in the elevator, and more.

If you found, let's say, 30 business events in the **Project Scope Blitz**, you'll have to schedule 30 different **detailed Discovery Sessions**. To do this right away is not reasonable, so ... don't do it. Based on the priorities established, I usually schedule no more than 3 or 4 at a time. This lets some of the dust settle as we discover details of the processes needed to support the different business events.

Graphically, it looks like this.

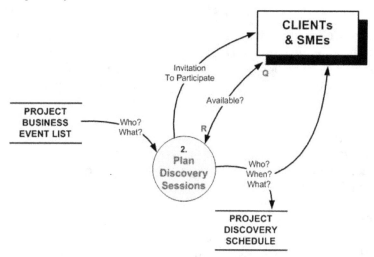

The planning process is as follows:

1. Based on the **Project Business Event List** you produced from the **Project Scope Blitz**, determine the availability of clients and subject-matter experts to participate in the detailed client-interactive Discovery Sessions for the project.

2. Create a **Project Discovery Schedule**, with participants and dates, for each *business event* on the **Project Business Event List**. Don't plan your entire list. That will only cause chaos, confusion and lots of rework later on. Just do 3 or 4 at a time.

3. When the schedule is complete (for 3 or 4 at a time), issue the Project Discovery Schedule and a formal "Invitation to Participate" in the detailed Discovery Sessions to affected clients and subject-matter experts.

Follow-up with everyone by phone (not just email or text) or with a personal meeting. It is very important that participants feel these Discovery Sessions are crucially important and their success depends very much on their active participation.

For each *business event* in the project, you will need to schedule a single **detailed Discovery Session** for one (1) hour with clients and subject-matter experts, regardless of the perceived complexity (or simplicity) of the process needed to support the *business event*.

Your plan should provide for an additional three (3) hours per *business event* to complete all the documentation. This is because there may be remaining work to be done outside the actual Discovery Session.

These metrics are based on over 850 projects our consultants have done, and the numbers are solid and predictable. The one (1) hour interactive session with clients and subject-matter experts tends to be quite precise, particularly when these sessions are led by an analyst who has more experience conducting these sessions. The three (3) additional hours per *business event* to flesh out and complete the remaining documentation is the average, but we have found it varies from 30 minutes to several hours more, depending on complexity and the type of project. However, by planning for three (3) additional hours per *business event*, you'll be right on target at the end.

An "average" project, we have found, is between 25-75 *business events*. A "small" project is less than 25 *business events*. And a "large" one is over 75 *business events*.

Based on needing one hour of discovery time per *business events*, a "small" project will take up less than 25 hours of clients and subject-matter experts. An "average" project needs between 25 and 75 hours with clients and subject-matter experts. And a "large" project needs over 75 hours of their time.

If necessary, this can all be scheduled one hour at a time, over an extended period. For mission critical projects, detailed Discovery Sessions for a project can also be scheduled as one hour per *business event* on consecutive days, with all parties involved. This "complete immersion" approach is very effective (arguably the most effective approach), but also very exhausting for subject-matter experts and the business analysts. We must also consider that clients and SMEs have their own work to do, and dedicating several full days to Discovery Sessions is usually difficult.

Regardless of the approach you take – and I do recommend the scheduling of one-hour sessions – each *business event* needs an average of three (3) additional hours by the analyst to dig up more details with subject-matter experts, and to complete the business requirements specification for each *business event*.

The detailed Discovery Session is a team activity (you and a co-pilot on one team; and clients and subject-matter experts on the other); therefore, typical teamwork guidelines apply. It usually takes a project team a couple of days of detailed Discovery Sessions to jell and to ramp up on foundation information.

What kind of facility is required?

Any room with lots of uncluttered wall space will do. The wall space is important so you can put *Write On – Cling On* sheets on them to draw the diagrams you need, so everyone in the room can see what has been done. While there is lots of technology that can project the diagrams onto a screen or a wall, including Smart Boards, we have found the dynamics and comfort level of participants when using *Write On – Cling On* sheets and whiteboards can't be duplicated.

Participants should be seated comfortably with desk or table space.

Who should participate?

A detailed Discovery Session should include a number of key people. Each Discovery Session should include clients and subject-matter experts who are crucial to the success of the project, including senior managers, other business partners with a stake in the project, project 'primes' and anyone else who has a good understanding of the project's objectives, business rationale, and re-engineering vision.

A business and its systems can only be as good as the dedication and participation shown by its owners and stakeholders. All participants in a Detailed Discovery session must bring an open mind. These Discovery Sessions enable participants to "liberate the mind" and potentially discover business re-engineering opportunities, including immediate opportunities for improvement. (An *Immediate Opportunity for Improvement*, or 'IOI', is an opportunity discovered during requirements analysis that can be acted upon almost immediately and can lead to substantial business process improvement and added value to the business.) These IOI's, often uncovered in Discovery Sessions, can be invaluable to an agile organization.

Participants in detailed discovery sessions should include the following:

Discovery Session Leader – The Pilot. The "Pilot" is an experienced business system analyst who leads and facilitates Discovery Sessions. I like to use the term "Pilot" because he or she must lead the session, keep it on course, and take it to its desired destination without problems.

Without a doubt, the "Pilot" is most instrumental to the success of the detailed Discovery Session, and the successful "Pilot" has an exceptional combination of skills.

- The "Pilot" must have excellent communication and cooperation skills.

- The "Pilot" must be able to deal with political disputes, power struggles and personality clashes, although this doesn't happen very often.

- The "Pilot" needs to be completely impartial, with no political baggage, and be able to keep an open mind while managing conversations.

- The "Pilot" must be sensitive to hidden agendas and be able to redirect them constructively.

- The "Pilot" must be able to bridge communication gaps – technical, linguistic and cultural.

- The "Pilot" must be comfortable speaking to and managing a group of people that often includes senior executives.

- The "Pilot" must encourage quiet group members to contribute their thoughts, and manage positively strong personalities that sometimes dominate sessions.

Achieving all of this is not for the faint-of-heart. Therefore, the "Pilot" must have the respect of those who participate in Discovery Sessions. That respect is earned through a series of successful Discovery Sessions, but it also comes from general comportment, dress, civility, respect for participants, and being non-judgmental of contributions.

My experience is that when a requirements Discovery Sessions fails, it is almost always because of the session leader or facilitator.

One of the reasons for session failure is when an organization wants to train a large number of people as "Pilots", but they lack sufficient recognition of the value of experience. Some managers (thankfully, not too many) believe they can assign a new "Pilot" to a project immediately after a candidate has finished an analysis course. Unfortunately, the result of trying to get everyone up to speed immediately, without the blessings and pain of experience, is that almost no one gets there. This, in turn, can lead to unskilled "Pilots" and weak results. Weak results can lead to backsliding to the endless search for an analysis methodology "that works". Of course, the methodology works just fine; problems are usually the result of "Pilot" error.

It is my opinion that an organization that intends to use this approach to business system analysis should train, and support, a small core group of expert "Pilot" practitioners. These "Pilots" should conduct as many Discovery Sessions throughout the year as possible. Our experience is that it takes about four projects for a new "Pilot" to become reasonably proficient. And it quickly gets better after that.

Expert Scribe – The Co-Pilot. The "co-pilot" must truly be *expert*. The "co-pilot" can't just be the next available body. They must be fully trained in business requirements analysis and how a Discovery Sessions is run. They must know what they are hearing when they hear it; such as Objects, data attributes and business rules. And they must have the knowledge and ability to back up the "Pilot", if required. We call this person a 'co-pilot' for just that reason.

The primary role of the "co-pilot" is to record what is said and done in the detailed Discovery Sessions. As such, this person will actively participate to make sure everything that's said and done is clear and concise.

Sometimes a "Pilot" is their own "co-pilot". Yes, really. This is the famous "team" of one person. It means the Pilot/Co-pilot wears a different hat at different times. However, if a "Pilot" is supported by a different person acting as "co-pilot", the time it takes to complete all the requirements documentation for the project is about half of what's needed if the "Pilot" works alone as both "Pilot" and "co-pilot".

An Expert Coach. For the first four projects we recommend that an analyst be supported by an expert coach: Someone who is expert at running these Discovery Sessions and business requirements analysis. Having a coach who is experienced with these Discovery Sessions will lead to mastery of the methods and project success much faster, and with fewer challenges. This approach is a common practice in almost all professions and trades. It is time that we assured our own success by applying this best practice.

Executive Sponsors and Project Primes. If you want the project to succeed, make sure an executive sponsor or a fully empowered project prime participate in the **Project Scope Blitz**. The absence of these people sends the message that the project isn't important enough for participation by other business partners and subject-matter experts. Executive sponsors and project primes are not necessarily the best people to participate in detailed Discovery Sessions, unless they are clear subject-matter experts.

Subject-Matter Experts and other Business Partners. Get them involved as much as possible and as quickly as possible. Involve the client directly, as well as the subject-matter experts. Involve as many of the key people from the affected business areas and department as quickly as you can. They should have a deep interest and enthusiasm for the success of the project. They should be the decision-makers, as well as the subject-matter experts (and are sometimes the same people). Their knowledge of the business and their vision is instrumental to the success of the sessions.

Why do we need to do this?

Alright, why do we need to do this, when we could just conduct traditional interviews, or run good old fashioned JAD sessions?

First, interviews are impossible to make work effectively. They take too long, sometimes are impossible to complete with all the subject-matter experts on a project, and almost never enable cross-learning opportunities on new projects, thus enabling business process reengineering. Traditional interviews are dead in the water, in my opinion.

Second, good old-fashioned JAD sessions as simply that: Old-fashioned, and much too rigid in approach. They are also much too focused on design by committee, rather than trying to figure out what the actual business requirements are.

Detailed Discovery Sessions accomplish any number of things, including the following:

(1) They enable better management of client expectations – because the client is directly and actively involved in specifying the business requirements right up front. Since their involvement in producing the requirements is direct, and not just as "approvers" of the resulting document, they take ownership of the product based on the idea that most people don't disagree with themselves.

(2) They enable effective and efficient transfer of business knowledge from the client or subject-matter expert to the business analyst – again, because of the client's direct involvement.

(3) Discovery Sessions enable identification of important business *conditions, situations* or *circumstances* not previously mentioned or recognized by the client. These *business events* that were not previously recognized as within the scope of the project can include new opportunities for business revitalization not previously expected by the client.

(4) Discovery Sessions facilitate client 'buy-in' since they are directly involved in the discovery process of establishing the essential business processes, the data required to support those processes, and key business rules that govern the required behavior of the system.

(5) Client-interactive Discovery Sessions dramatically reduce the amount of time spent on identifying key business requirements.

(6) Client-interactive Discovery Sessions reduce acquisition, development and implementation time considerably by removing ambiguity and ensuring fewer revisions (caused by omission) to the final system. In other words, it's faster by involving the clients and subject-matter experts right up front, and basing their involvement on individual *business events*.

(7) A client-interactive Discovery Session approach is essentially a **single-iteration approach**. What this means is that after one fast Discovery Session with subject-matter experts for each *business event* in the target system, your business requirements specification will be complete – within the framework of the 80/20 Rule. No further revisiting, reiteration, rediscovery or redefinition of business requirements is necessary. A single-iteration (once through) approach to business system requirements means your analysis efforts are as fast as possible. This truly is the definition of "agile" within a no-risk paradigm.

So, what is a business event?

I've said a lot about *business events* in the context of Discovery Sessions. I can't just leave it there … so, let's discuss what a *business event* really is.

A *business event* is an essential business condition, a state, circumstance, situation or requirement that exists – which the target system must respond to or deal with in order to successfully support its key business objectives. A *business event* transcends time and technology; i.e., it does not reflect *how* something is done; it represents *what* must be done without regard to a particular technology.

To summarize, a *business event* is:

• a state, condition, circumstance, situation or requirement that exists;
• essential (critical) to the business; and

- based on time, a decision, situation or third party need.

The Four Types of Business Events

Business events come in four flavors:

1) **Situation Business Event** – non-controlled
   "The Customer Buys a Product"
   "The Customer Has Exceeded Their Credit Limit"

2) **External Business Event** – based on third party need
   "The Customer Requests a Higher Credit Limit"

3) **Temporal Business Event** – based on time
   "The Customer's Credit Card Expires"
   "It is Time to Increase the Customer's Credit Limit"

4) **Internal Business Event** – based on a decision
   "The Company Decides to Cancel the Customer's Credit Card"

Note that a *business event* **never** starts with a verb. That's because a *business event* is not a process. A *business event* is a condition, state, situation or circumstance that must be supported by a process.

For clarity – when a *business event* is identified we don't label it as one of the four kinds of *business events* listed above. We leave it unlabeled because, to a client or anyone else who is reading the documentation, a *business event* is simply a *business event*. It's a business circumstance. The four categories of *business events* exist to help the analyst to think about what kind of situation or circumstance they are really dealing with.

For example, what's the difference between **"The Company Decides to Pay a Supplier"** and **"It is Time to Pay a Supplier"**?

The first one (an internal *business event* based on a decision) suggests that there is a decision point, and this decision must be reflected in the requirements document. The second one (an internal *business event* based on time) suggests that there is no decision involved, it's just <u>time</u> to pay the supplier – perhaps the goods ordered have been received, or it's 30 days, and it is therefore time to pay the supplier.

By assessing the type of *business event*, the analyst is able to think through the ramifications on the business requirements.

The most common type of *business event* used by those who are new to this kind of analysis is the temporal *business event* that starts with **"It Is Time to ..."**. While this truly is a common type of *business event*, it is also the most common error, mostly because it is so easy to identify a *business event* as **"It Is Time to ... (something)"**.

For example, I have often seen *business events* such as **"It Is Time to Receive a Product Shipment from a Supplier"** when it clearly should be **"Product Shipment Arrives from a Supplier"**. The arrival of the shipment from the supplier, while expected, is somewhat out of our control, therefore it is an external *business event*. To state **"It Is Time to Receive a Product Shipment from a Supplier"** seems a bit awkward and certainly doesn't have the same meaning as **"Product Shipment Arrives from a Supplier"**. On the other hand, a *business event* such as, **"It Is Time for a Product Shipment from a Supplier to Arrive"** is something else again. This kind of *business event* is within our control, and we must have a planned response for it.

Thinking through the type of *business event* we're dealing with is therefore helpful in stating it well.

The Symbiotic Relationship between Objects and Processes.

Anyone who leads a detailed Discovery Session must not only uncover the project's *business events*, but must also be listening for the data required, so they can eventually develop the business process to support the *business event*.

Let's talk about that for a moment, since this all has to do with running awesome Discovery Sessions.

A business "process" is inseparable from "data" – they have a genuine symbiotic relationship. In other words, each *business event* (i.e., circumstance or condition) that needs to be supported by the target system (or business area) must be <u>dealt with by that target system in some manner</u> (i.e., a specific process). This always requires <u>the use of data</u> – either to retrieve some data or to record some data. It's impossible to have a process that doesn't involve retrieving, viewing or recording of data. It's equally redundant to have data that isn't ever involved in some kind of process – something has to happen to it, otherwise why do we bother recording it?

So, for each business event, there must be a related business process. The business process must identify the data needed to support it.

For a full and complete discussion of a methodology to find and describe business processes and accompanying data, you can read my book *"Rapid, Agile Business System Analysis: Fast, Agile, Measurable Results"*, which can be found on Amazon.

Here are the steps any leader of a Discovery Session should go through:

Create a short list of potential *business events* for the project.

Identify as many as possible. Send me an email, and I'll send you a list of almost 4,000 business events from over 850 projects, organized by category.

After an initial list of potential *business events* has been created, pick one *business event* to start with and ask the subject-matter experts (the ones who have knowledge in the context of the chosen *business event*) the following question:

"What do we need to <u>know about</u> or <u>remember</u> in order to support this business condition or circumstance?"

The purpose of this question is to discover what data is needed to support the *business event*. To then find the data, we can do the following:

Look and listen for nouns.

The first place you can look is in the *business event* statement itself. It will consist of at least a verb and a noun or more. The nouns in the *business event* statement are usually data Objects.

Listen for nouns with "substance".

A data Object that supports a business process must have at least two data items. Less is just a data attribute. For example, would the noun "**CUSTOMER**" need several data items to describe it? Would we need to know the *customer's name*, *address*, *phone number*, and more? If so – and if there are at least two such attributes and characteristics – then we have a real data Object. If not, then we just have an attribute that belongs to some other data Object.

It follows that all nouns are not data Objects. Some are just data attributes that belong to and describe data Objects. Others are full data Objects. To know the difference you must determine if the piece of data, the noun, can be further decomposed. If you can't further decompose it, it's a data attribute. If you can, it's a data Object. And data Objects are the "data" that's described in any business process.

Identify data attributes by listening for nouns that are not Objects.

Sometimes we just don't know where a data item belongs, simply because it's a stray with no identifiable home (another data Object). When a client mentions a series of nouns that are clearly data items but don't seem to belong to a data Object already defined, but are also undoubtedly related – such as *customer name*, *address*, *phone number* – then we "roll up" a group of related data items to form a new data Object that hasn't yet been formed.

Ask the Inclusion Question (for Objects).

For every data Object that participates in a process that supports a *business event* ask the following question:

"If I know about {the OBJECT} what will it <u>enable</u> us to do that we could not do if we didn't know about it?"

Ask the Exclusion Question (for Objects).

For every data Object that participates in a process that supports a *business event* ask the following question:

"If we <u>do not know</u> about {the OBJECT} what will it <u>prevent</u> us from doing that we must be able to do?"

Each of these questions is asked in a client-interactive requirements Discovery Session. Discovery Sessions with subject-matter experts are very similar to technical JAD sessions, but Discovery Sessions focus entirely on the business requirements and not on system solutions or design. **J**oint **A**pplication **D**esign (or Development) is a session in which subject-matter experts and system developers interact to determine <u>system</u> functionality and output. In business Discovery Sessions, answers to questions asked of subject-matter experts by a Pilot are captured by the co-pilot (an expert scribe) for each process that supports a *business event*.

Discovery Sessions with subject-matter experts are conducted on the basis of one or more specific *business events*. For each *business event*, you will create some kind of business process diagram. It really doesn't matter what kind, as long as you are comfortable and your client community are also comfortable with your diagrams. You'll do the process diagram, identify supporting data Objects, populate the data Objects with data items, and determine business rules specific to the business process. All of this will be done with the direct interactive participation and contribution of your subject-matter experts.

And then we're done ...

As soon as possible after you've wrapped up a Discovery Session with subject-matter experts, and you have cleaned up all the resulting specifications and documentation – issue the business requirements dealing with the *business event* to all the stakeholders and subject-matter experts who participated in your Discovery Session.

"As soon as possible" could be the same day, but it's certainly within a day or two. The sooner it's done, the more responsive you'll be seen to be, and the more enthusiastic the response from your subject-matter experts will be too.

Three things are important in this very agile and lean process.

First – your documentation for a single *business event* should be very small. Typically, you will want to be asking them to review just 3 or 4 pages. You'll lose them if you have much more than that. It will consist of about two pages describing the process that supports the *business event*. Put the process diagram on one page (left) and the process narrative on the other page (right), if it doesn't fit under the diagram. For each of the data Objects you identify in the process diagram, you need to have a definition, data attributes and whatever business rules apply. Since most process diagrams only have 3 or 4 Objects, usually not more than six, this makes the documentation pretty lean. Once you've got this done for a process that supports a single, specific *business event*, send it to the subject-matter experts who participated in the Discovery Session. Ask them to read and review the document. Give them a deadline for feedback. Ask, clearly, that what you have sent them represents what you and your subject-matter experts discussed in the Discovery Session.

Second – what your subject-matter experts receive should look exactly like the process diagrams you drew in the actual

Discovery Session, just a little prettier ... so they will recognize what they are reviewing. Most of them will be very comfortable with this, since you have already spent some time on the business process and the business rules in the Discovery Session. Also, all the information contained in the very slim document is their knowledge, not yours. They will recognize it as such.

Third – your fast and timely distribution of the documentation means it's still fresh in their minds. As they read, they will recall what was discussed. This provides the continuity you need to get good feedback. It will also stimulate them to get the feedback back to you as quickly as possible.

I have found this to be an exceptionally fast, agile and lean way of getting good feedback quickly, and a good way of keeping subject-matter experts involved past the actual interactive Discovery Sessions. It's a way of overcoming the "out of sight, out of mind" syndrome, which can have so much effect of project progress.

What tools can you use for documentation?

Let's get one issue out of the way. I am not a supporter of certain software (you know the kind) because every one of these applications is designed to help software engineers, not your business partners. What they see and what they get is totally alien to their own business world.

In terms of what works well, the most commonly used is still simple documents, emailed internally. But Wikis are definitely popular too. I certainly recommend the use of an expert-moderated Wiki for any project.

Wikis are easy-to-use, collaborative and do not need to be serial. Different users can work on different parts of the Wiki at different times. You can restrict access to anyone individuals or groups you want. The most famous Wiki is of course Wikipedia, which really is a collaboration on thousands of projects.

A Business Area or Project Wiki is particularly good for teams that are dispersed across the country, around the world, or even in different offices across the city. Feedback can be almost instant, and knowledge can be contributed by the people who have the knowledge.

A Project Wiki has two lives. The first is when it is the knowledge repository consisting of the business requirements specification preceding software installation. The second is its life after the software is implemented. The transition from a business requirement Wiki to a Business Area or a Project Wiki takes place when stakeholders and subject-matter experts start to maintain the knowledge contained in the business requirements as a knowledge set of the business areas. Since this includes all areas and interfaces, not just those features developed as software support, the Project Wiki becomes a teaching and learning tool for the affected business areas.

The intent of any Project Wiki is to make changes easy to do, not difficult. Traditional documentation is always difficult to maintain, and is never maintained very well, if at all. Traditional documentation, once it is completed, is often never looked at again. That's a terrible waste. And it's very costly to the project in the future.

When a Business Area or Project Wiki is developed this way, maintenance of the business documentation now becomes the responsibility of the client and the subject-matter experts in the different business areas.

Key Success Factors

So, let's talk about some of the things that will help you make a successful project.

There are many success factors that are unique to each particular Discovery Session. However, there are some generally accepted success factors that apply to just about any kind of interactive session:

- Be sure that the project's executive sponsors and key stakeholders attend and actively participate in the initial *Project Scope Blitz*.

- Issue the <u>Project Business Event List</u> to everyone who participated in the *Project Scope Blitz* as soon as possible after the session is done. It should go out no later than a day after the session.

- Set realistic expectations for the work to be done in the detailed Discovery Sessions, and a realistic schedule. In terms of the time required, plan on one (1) hour per *business event*, with clients and subject-matter experts (SMEs) participating, and an additional three (3) hours per *business events* to complete the analysis and documentation. That will be fast, and realistic.

  As I mentioned earlier, you may not actually need the addition three hours for every single *business event*. For some, you'll be able to clean it up and get it ready for distribution in less than 30 minutes, but for others it could take 6 or even 12 hours, depending on what you discover in your post-Discovery Session assessment. The three hours is an average over all the *business events*. Therefore, if you have 30 *business events*, you'll need 30 one-hour Discovery Sessions with SMEs, and a total of 90 additional hours of finishing work. This metric, the result of tracking over 850 projects, enables you to make a reasonable estimate of time required immediately after finishing a Project Scope Blitz. That's a whole lot better than an out-and-out guess based on nothing better than thin air, a prayer and a song.

- Be very visible by conducting Discovery Sessions with all the people required to be involved in a *business event*. Avoid one-person interviews. They are inefficient, take much too long, and hide your visibility. Visibility demonstrates that you are not only gathering the requirements, but you are *seen* to be gathering the requirements.

- If the project becomes a software acquisition or development project, make sure the software engineers (the programmers, database designers and system designers) know how to read the kind of Business Requirements Document you will produce; and, if custom building the software, how to turn it into a solution design.

- Do a lot of Discovery Sessions, every chance you get; but perfect practice – with a coach and mentor for "Pilots" and "co-pilots" – works better than practice without guidance by an expert. Having a coach experienced in these kinds of Discovery Sessions will lead to mastery of the methods much faster, and project success with fewer challenges.

Other general success factors include:

- Actively encourage everyone to participate. Instead of being just a facilitator, be a proactive "Pilot" and leader.

- Have well established and agreed upon objectives for each Discovery Session. Explain to participants how a Discovery Session will generally only deal with the specific *business event* scheduled and the business process, data Objects, and business rules needed to support it. Explain how you may find some new, previously undiscovered *business events*, but these will not be dealt with in their own Discovery Sessions. New *business events* discovered will be added to the Project Business Event (Parking Lot) and will be done at some later time in the schedule.

- Be unbiased and neutral about the business requirement. As a business system analyst it is your responsibility to determine what the client needs to support the business. It is **not** the business analyst's function to assess the correctness or value of the client's requirements. (Some will disagree with me on this, but that's OK; they are allowed to be wrong.) While you may suggest a path for your subject-matter experts (by using questions rather than answers), it is the client's responsibility to determine the business processes and data that add value to the business.

- "Keep it as simple as possible, but no simpler." (With thanks to Albert Einstein.)

- Keep focused on the objectives. Stay with the subject *business event*, and don't jump to other unplanned subjects. Use the <u>Project Business Event List (Parking Lot)</u> for new *business events* that come up in discussion.

- Lead the discovery process. Facilitate the requirements.

- Use the client's terminology. No technobabble.

- Don't judge the client's questions and answers. If you didn't understand what they said, or if it just sounded strange, ask them to help you understand their question or answer.

- Never fear that your questions will sound strange or uninformed. I've found that this is actually a good thing, even when I have to pretend to understand less than I actually do. People love to tell you about what they do and their responsibilities. They also love to tell you what they know. And that's what Discovery Session are all about: getting the expert knowledge from the subject-matter experts.

- Challenge the SME's thinking, but do not challenge the SME. Sounds good, but how do you do that? The first step is to never ask *"Why?"* when they give you an answer. "Why?" is not a good question to ask an adult. In effect, it asks them to justify or rationalize their answer, and they are not there to do that. If a senior manager says, *"We want a report on widgets sold in the northwest region,"* and you're not quite certain what this means, it's not a good idea to ask that manager *"Why?"* The answer you get is probably not what you're looking for. Instead, replace your desire to ask "Why?" with the following question: *"John, if we have the report on widget sales in the northwest region, what will that <u>enable</u> us to do that we have to be able to do?"* ... or, from another perspective, *"John, if we <u>don't</u> have the report on widget sales in the northwest region, what will that <u>prevent</u> us from doing that we must be able to do?"* You'll get a real answer with either of these questions (which are just two sides of the same coin). The answer you get will be the real *business event* that you're looking for.

- Be clear and understandable. Don't mumble. Use complete sentences consisting of both nouns and verbs, at least most of the time. Don't use technobabble or terms the subject-matter experts are not familiar with. Avoid using acronyms unless they are common to your industry (which means many others besides yourself must know the acronym).

- Make people feel good. The better they feel, the more readily they will participate in future Discovery Session. Be good finding.

- Smile. A lot. People respond a whole lot better to smiles, especially if the subject is serious and sometimes complicated.

- Have fun. Use your good sense of humor. If this is sometimes difficult for you, work on developing a sense of humor. It can be learned and become part of your personality.

- Listen... listen... and listen some more. What people say and what they mean are sometimes a little different. Keep really focused on what they mean. When you're not sure, ask them to *"help me understand that better"*.

- If you are asked a question, you must <u>always</u> respond to the participant's answer in some manner.

These are some of the key success factors. Undoubtedly, there are many others that apply equally well.

Discovery Sessions Tips and Techniques

These are some of the key success factors. Undoubtedly, there are many others that apply equally well.

On the Discovery Sessions

- When starting a detailed Discovery Session, remember to ground the participants in the fact that you will be focusing on the **'WHAT'**, not the **'HOW'**. Keep reminding them of this if they drift into how things should be done (solution design) or other solution discussions.

- There's a basic principle I like to remind everyone about: *"Partition the effort to minimize complexity."* If the process underlying a *business event* is becoming too complex, and if your brain is about to explode, it's probably because the subject-matter experts are attempting to have a single process support several *business events*. While this is natural, try to keep it as simple as possible. Simple works. Don't try to make it more complex. Go with it until you know better. Don't speculate about what you don't know. Peggy Lee, a wonderful jazz singer from the day, once made the song *"Is That All There Is?"* very famous. Yes, often, that is all there is. Move on.

- Optics is important in Discovery Sessions. So, print legibly on the whiteboards or *Write On – Cling On* sheets, and use **red** and **blue** as alternating colors when drawing pictures during a Discovery Session. It helps with visual recognition of material for your subject-matter experts, the "co-pilot", and you, the "Pilot". Stay away from the other colors, since most of them can't be seen very well from even a few feet away.

- After you've completed some kind of <u>Business Process Diagram</u> with your subject-matter experts, walk through (or talk through) the process as a wrap-up, so your SMEs can confirm its substance once again. It also enables your co-pilot to validate that everything has been recorded accurately.

- As the Pilot, periodically check to ensure that the co-pilot is keeping up with you. Before a detailed Discovery Session, work out signals between the two of you so the co-pilot can indicate a need to catch up before moving forward.

- As the Pilot, listen for the co-pilot's fingers hitting the keyboard. If there is dead silence, take a break from the Discovery Session and speak with your co-pilot to determine if everything is OK – that the co-pilot is actually capturing the information as it arises during the Discovery Session. Also listen for the pace of keying; i.e., is the co-pilot still keying something while you are ready to move ahead to the next topic. Or, has keying stopped and it appears the co-pilot is also ready to move on. Team communication is as important between you and your co-pilot as it is between you and your SMEs. If you are your own co-pilot (sigh), only speak to yourself in your inside voice.

- Tracking requirements in a system can be done by identifying specific data items in data Objects that define a particular status (e.g., open, closed, approved, rejected, etc.). Attributing a *date/time* data item to each different status will provide a complete record of an instance of a data Object as it changes state in a system.

- Remember that an "inventory" is really a list of many instances of a particular data Object (like "PRODUCT"), each having its own unique identifier (key). If you are looking at inventory management *business events*, consider having a status data item in the data Object (e.g., *sold, available, returned*, etc.) with an associated <u>*date/time*</u>. This will easily provide the information needed to create reports, issue product reorders, etc.

- Avoid using soft words when discussing business processes in a Discovery Session. Soft words like "update," "modify," "process," and "handle" are words that are only meaningful (i.e., have a clear definition) to the speaker. Instead, use pointier words like "record" and "remember".

- Always remember to get your SMEs to provide a concise definition of a data Object. It ensures everyone has the same understanding of what the data Object represents. Interestingly, data Object definitions expand considerably during most detailed Discovery Sessions, so don't be happy with the first definition you encounter. It will probably change as you progress with the Discovery Sessions.

- Always think of a data Object in the singular. It helps ground people in understanding the purpose of the business process without getting distracted by number of instances, time, etc. Also, we (people) are not very good at thinking through multiplicity. Stick to the singular.

- Always name a data Object in the singular, even though it represents all possible occurrences of the data Object, including its history. Your diagrams represent the business view of the information, not a database design view.

On the Co-Pilot

The co-pilot is as important to the success of a Discovery Session as the Pilot. They have different but equally important roles. The following notes are for co-pilots who work with Pilots by documenting everything as it happens during a detailed discovery session.

So, if you're a project co-pilot, here's some advice based on hundreds of projects' experience.

- **Have the Pilot explain your role.**

  Initially, as a co-pilot, people will wonder why you are there and what you are recording. Will their words be held against them? Are you a spy? Clarify that you are there to ensure that the information discovered during this session is appropriately documented. Let participants know that a Business Requirements Document will be produced as soon as possible after all the Discovery Sessions are done. If the Business Requirements Document, or some part of it will be distributed, let them know that too.

- **Listen, listen, and listen some more.**

  Often, there will be more than one conversation taking place. The challenge is to figure out which is the key one. Try to stay focused on the same dialogue as the Pilot is engaged in. Because the Pilot will likely be actively listening to a specific discussion, encourage others to speak up (at the right time) if you are aware of other side discussions taking place.

- **Seek clarification.**

  If there is something you don't understand, ask for clarification. Most people in the room don't expect you to be an expert in the business at hand. That's their job. Your role is to ensure that the facts, as well as the thoughts and concerns of the SMEs get appropriately documented. Consequently, if you do not understand, or if the discussion has gone off in several directions, it is absolutely appropriate to ask participants to repeat their words to ensure that the discussion is accurately documented.

  However, as the expert co-pilot, there is an expectation that you will have some innate ability to hear all, understand all, and document all. Sometimes you may find that it is more appropriate to follow up with specific individuals off line. Your good judgment is necessary.

- **Read back complex narratives or business rules for confirmation.**

  If a particularly complex business process has been under discussion for some time, it may be appropriate to request a break so that you can consolidate your notes. If you do, after the break read back the updated version of the narrative or the business rules to get everyone back onto the same page.

- **Define all acronyms.**

  If acronyms are used in the discovery session (and they almost always are), make a note of them and follow up with individuals off line to ensure complete understanding. Ensure that full definitions of these terms are included at least once in the document. If appropriate, consider adding a glossary of acronyms as an appendix.

- **If participants wish to see what you're doing, share it with them on breaks.**

  Remember, the document you are preparing belongs to everyone in the room. It is the consolidation of all their thoughts, ideas and experience. If they want to grab a glimpse on a break, no problem; share it with them. This is an excellent opportunity to check with individuals one-on-one to validate specific comments in the document. This will also enhance their confidence that their words are being recorded appropriately and that a great deal of work is being done by you, the scribing co-pilot, as well as by the people in the room. Visibility comes in many ways.

- **Leave the diagrams for later.**

  A Business Process Diagram will likely change as you progress through the Discovery Session. Diagrams are often on whiteboards or on *Write On – Cling On* sheets on the wall. Once again, visibility of the work you do is very important. Use the diagrams to get the process narratives correct during the session. Once the process definition and diagram are stable, add the diagram to your documentation.

After the Discovery Sessions

- **Add the diagrams to your documentation.**

  Copy the diagrams from the whiteboards or *Write on – Cling On* sheets on the walls to your documentation during the consolidation period at the end of the day, when there are no clients or subject-matter experts around. Since diagrams can change during a discovery session as you get more information, there will be no time for you to capture the diagrams (perhaps more than once) during the session.

- **Create a backup of the diagrams.**

  Before you move any of the diagrams on *Write On – Cling On* sheets, create backup copies by using your trusty digital camera or Smartphone. Take photos of all the diagrams.

Other thoughts ...

Where appropriate, give key subject-matter experts an opportunity to "see" an early version of the documentation for a specific Business Process Diagram (which may support one or more *business events*). This gives them a sense of how much work is actually getting done. Visibility is one of the keys to success.

When reviewing specific documentation with a subject-matter expert, be prepared for some "wordsmithing". This is why you are reviewing it – to ensure that the way the information is documented is how they want it. "Wordsmithing" is a step in the ownership process.

As discussed earlier, consider posting individual processes and their supporting information as part of an internal Project Wiki. The business processes should represent what the organization wants, without detailing how it will be delivered, and it should be a living document. As a Project Wiki (or a Business Area Wiki), it can be used by the client community as a teaching or training tool, and it can easily be maintained by the client community that owns the business processes.

More Tips and Techniques ...

Listening

During the detailed Discovery Session, concentrate on listening to what is being said. Business Process Diagrams and Object data attributes can be captured at the end of the day – they'll still be on the *Write On – Cling On* sheets when all the subject-matter experts have left. Also, most narratives can be constructed from a good diagram quite easily. Look to the data flows to find the tasks.

There is a lot said during the Discovery Session by the Pilot and by the SMEs themselves that will not appear on any diagram you create, but needs to be captured in your narratives. Concentrate on combining what you see on your diagrams with what you've heard, and you should be able to build a process narrative that accurately describes the process taking place.

Judgment

A large part of being an expert Pilot or co-pilot is being able to determine what needs to be captured, and to distinguish the needed data from other information that arises during the discussion. Many times in a Discovery Session a SME will get caught up in an explanation that contains a lot of information which is not really applicable to the immediate work you are doing. You are not there to capture full descriptions of the job functions of everybody in the room. You only want to capture information that belongs to the project's business requirements. Any extraneous information captured means there is that much more for the readers of the document to wade through to get to the real requirements. And that's not a good thing.

However, you simply can't cut somebody off and tell them that the information they are providing, while it might be important, is not useful in the document. Use common sense, and be flexible. Sometimes, letting someone get off-track in an area they believe to be important, can actually be very productive. Listening is a proactive skill that also requires the good judgment to let someone be heard, even when there's not much direct value added.

Verification

Don't be afraid to interrupt, stop the discussion, and insure that what you've captured is what has been said. The information that you are capturing must represent what was said – you are building the definitive record of the business requirements. If you're not sure, double-check with the people that know best – the subject-matter experts.

If you're the co-pilot (and you're not part of that magical team-of-one when your also the Pilot), be sure to discuss your 'interruption option' with the Pilot before the Discovery Session starts. Agree on the best way to verify your information where required, and try to stick to that method. Don't step on any toes. However, do not interrupt the discussion to add your own two cents worth regarding the business process. As the co-pilot you are not one of the subject-matter experts – that's why they are in the room.

If you have a vested interest in the outcome of the session, do not agree to be the co-pilot. If you're talking, you can't be listening or recording, and you'll very quickly find that you're falling behind in the capture of information. Your writing will also be biased, even if it is unintentional.

Teamwork

If you're the co-pilot, you and the Pilot are a team. Do your best to use your knowledge of business system analysis to know the direction in which the discussion could be heading, so you're not caught by surprise. Be ready to read back anything you've captured, at any time.

As a co-pilot, if you have any questions about what is drawn or annotated on a *Write On – Cling On* sheet, ask the Pilot right away.

Technical Details

The business requirements concern the "what" and not the "how". It is not a technical specification. It is a business specification. That being said, there are times during Discovery Session when there are things mentioned that might not be considered to be business requirements, but might be information that's needed to populate the database once it is complete.

For example, let's say you're discussing gas tanks. A data Object called GAS TANK would have attributes such as *height, width, depth, location, weight, date entered into inventory,* and *capacity*. One of the SMEs might say, *"Well, none of our tanks can hold more than 100 gallons. Ever."* Although this is a piece of technical data (which is certainly implementation dependent, since it could change in the future), it could save some time at a later point in the project if this fact is noted now, and it won't take long to record it as part of the business requirements. The way to get around the "physical" nature of this data is to just enter it as a note in the description of the data attribute (*capacity,* in this example).

Five Phrases

For the purpose of writing narratives for business processes, here are five phrases I have found invaluable to kick-start the building of a process narrative.

1. "For each ..."
2. "Periodically ..."
3. "Determine ..."
4. "Remember (or record) ..."

5. "Find (or identify) …"

Don't limit yourself to these particular phrases when building your narratives, but they may come in very handy if you find you can't think of how to word what you've just heard.

In addition to the word "Find" another word that might be helpful is "Identify". For example, when making a sale you want to remember who made the sale, but you don't need any sales person information and you don't need to record anything about the salesperson. In this case, you might simply write, "Identify the SALESPERSON who made the sale."

The Agile environment

The real key to being a successful expert co-pilot is to practice what you've learned. You'll find that the more you scribe, the better you'll be, and the easier it is to hear everything that's being said. You might even find, with lots of practice, that you can listen to two (or even three) conversations at the same time and pick out what's important in each of them. (Ideally, there should only ever be one conversation taking place in the room at the same time, but we all know that this isn't reality.)

Lastly, know the analysis methodology you're learning. Not just learn it, but know it. Internalize it. Because if you know how all of the information that you're hearing in a discovery session fits together, you'll spend much less time thinking about where to put what you've heard – and you'll miss less. Discovery Session participants will be absolutely amazed by how you can capture so much information, and that you can so accurately describe their business processes.

Above all, if you want to foster an agile environment, involve your clients and subject-matter experts in requirements discovery, and involve them a lot.

Your business requirements documentation should be in business language, and as brief as possible. And a client should not be expected to learn the technology you're using.

Recognize that you serve your client – whether that client is part of an internal group or a customer outside your organization – and you need their help and active participation to understand their requirements.

Recognize that requirements will change as your client understands better the information they want and can have. It's not a bad thing to "change your mind" when you have more information. As the famous British economist John Maynard Keynes once said, *"When the facts change, I change my opinion. What do you do?"* The issue is how to deal with those changes, since history tells us that change is good. This is what learning is all about, so when a client or subject-matter expert changes their mind, don't think *"not on my project."* This is actually a move in the right direction.

I believe very strongly that requirements analysis should be focused on individual *business events*, and their supporting processes, rather than trying to write a novel about how a system should work. By focusing on the individual *business event* and its supporting processes and data, you can respond very quickly to any change that is needed. It minimizes the complexity of changing page after page in a serial novel. In event-based analysis, as I've briefly described it, there is no redundancy; therefore, there is no domino effect in the documentation. It allows the business analyst to respond rapidly, while it gives the client or subject-matter expert the confidence to contribute without fear of criticism of "constantly changing their mind".

In my opinion, "agile" means being fast and responsive, but without chaos and risk. An event-based approach to business requirements analysis is extremely fast, and without risk. The alternative – conventional system analysis that usually takes a long time – often leads to abbreviated requirements analysis (*"we finished when we ran out of time"*), which in turn leads to incomplete work down the line, and perhaps costly rework later on.

The Professional's Success Code

Finally, let's talk about the professional's success code.

Bringing business professionals together with analysts in a modern and agile JAD-like requirements Discovery Session is the cornerstone of the environment you will create when doing business requirements analysis. This environment creates a dynamic and a "user buy-in" rarely seen before.

If you use highly client-interactive Discovery Sessions to help determine business requirements, my experience indicates that you will have great success uncovering business requirements quickly, accurately and completely. The size of your organization doesn't matter. It will work very well in virtually any size of organization, government or non-government, given motivated individuals.

To be successful on the projects we take on we must not only have a good requirements acquisition methodology – one that supports agility and responsiveness without chaos and risk – we must have an agile approach to business requirements analysis that is predictable and repeatable as well. What I mean by this is that every analyst who conducts Discovery Sessions should run them more or less the same way. So, cross-learning and internal mentorship is really important. This means that if different analysts conduct different Discovery Sessions on the same project, the results should have the same outputs and quality as if only one analyst was doing the work on a project.

Every professional must have a foundation that guides all system acquisition or development work. I believe the foundation can be best described as follows:

- **Be on budget, on time, no problems.**

The project manager or team leader must be committed to ensuring that the project is problem-free, on budget, and all deadlines are met. Since what is done up front determines all subsequent results, the fact that you conduct client-interactive Discovery Sessions help to make this objective possible.

- **Foster teamwork and client participation.**

The best relationship you can have with your clients is one of partnership, teamwork and active participation. The best results come when you work directly and visibly with your clients. Never work in isolation from them. Client-interactive Discovery Sessions help to make the partnership possible.

- **Apply hands-on modern management methods.**
- **Encourage on-project coaching and mentoring.**
- **Get management commitment to the project.**

Every project should be guided directly by a practicing expert in the tools, techniques and methodologies to be used on the project. It's a lot easier to advance when everyone is on board and understands how the work is actually done, rather than relying on theory passed on from an absentee practitioner or methodologist.

Management commitment and sponsorship is also enormously necessary to a project's success, as is a well-defined and developed professional development program for the business analysts and system developers. Client-interactive Discovery Sessions help to make all of this possible.

- **Be highly visible.**

My experience is that an informed and involved client will usually make the best decisions. We have found that visibility – contrary to popular myth – eliminates fear, uncertainty and doubt by the business community. Visibility always results in interaction and ownership. Don't hide from sight or work in isolation from your client. Have pride in your work. Success is the only option. Client-interactive Discovery Sessions help to make this possible.

- **Use best practices.**

Always use the best and most modern methods. This always results in faster results, less money being spent, and the highest quality. Always look for better ways. Avoid the *'Not Invented Here (NIH)'* syndrome. Look outside your organization. Be devoted to finding the best methods available. And then measure satisfaction by your client community. Client-interactive Discovery Sessions help to make this possible.

- **Apply the best methodologies.**

Use the most effective and pragmatic methodologies that you can find. Don't use them because they are popular, or the *solution du jour*; use them because they have an excellent track-record according to your clients and subject-matter experts. While I naturally suggest you use client-interactive Discovery Sessions on all your projects, big or small, adapt it as required to your organization, your industry, and your personal style of working. This will help you get the best results.

- **Use common sense – and a coach and mentor.**

A popular old saying is, *"common sense just isn't very common."* But I think it is. The first step is to get yourself a coach and mentor, and ask that person for some help whenever it's needed. Take a practical, common sense approach to all projects. Every situation is unique and each has different needs. Client-interactive Discovery Sessions help to make this possible too.

Come by and say hello.

Trond Frantzen
trond.frantzen@powerstartgroup.com
powerstartgroup.com